MOOLAH or BUMMER!

MOOLAH or BUMMER!

A Humorous Look at Finance and Investing

Moget Africa

iUniverse, Inc.

New York Lincoln Shanghai

MOOLAH or BUMMER!
A Humorous Look at Finance and Investing

iUniverse books may be ordered through booksellers or by contacting:

iUniverse
2021 Pine Lake Road, Suite 100
Lincoln, NE 68512
www.iuniverse.com
1-800-Authors (1-800-288-4677)

ISBN: 0-595-34431-3

Printed in the United States of America

For my mom and dad, for their many sacrifices,
and my children, for constantly inspiring me.

Contents

ACKNOWLEDGEMENTS

Without the encouragement of Lisa Garbrick, Hope Horton, Beverly Hudson and Jackie Leeson, this project would not have been completed. Thank you for prodding me (ever so gently and non-judgementally) to finish, and in the process, thank you for leading me to rediscover a part of me that has been long dormant. Thanks also to Tobin and Marc for their involvement in the early days of this project. As for the proverbial third grade teacher, I am like many other writers in this respect. Many thanks are owed to all my teachers from elementary through high school for the challenge of a blank page. Most of all, I thank my Mom (the original Moget) next to whom I spent many hours as a toddler happily creating "art" while she went about her chores. And to my Dad, thank you for all those early lessons in world business and finance. At age twelve I never quite understood your explanation of foreign exchange and stocks, but it sure sparked a lifelong interest.

INTRODUCTION

"Tonight for dinner we're having meatloaf and oh, by the way, did you hear about Apple's acquisition of...?" Sound like your mom or dad? If you're like most people, you didn't grow up with finance part of the dinner conversation. However, knowing instinctively the importance of financial stability, you're now playing catch-up. With that purpose in mind, many of us have visited a bookstore or library looking for a book that explains the basics of finance, especially everyday personal finance and investing. But if you're like most people, you probably skimmed several weighty tomes and found them "boring as hell" (no offense to the authors). You either abandoned your intentions or perhaps you were motivated enough to purchase a book. Well, have you read it? Or is it gathering dust like many good intentions?

Moolah or Bummer! A Humorous Look at Finance and Investing was created to introduce you to the basics of the financial language, especially if you don't have a formal financial education. Although CNBC and CNNfn have brought financial reporting into many living rooms, the terminology used by many reporters still assumes a basic level of proficiency. Well, *Moolah or Bummer!* will get you on board.

There are also many of us who shy away from finance and investing. The ups and downs of the markets, most recently the stock market bubble, reiterate the risk inherent in investing. However, power belongs to those who are informed and, if you're ever seen a bag-lady, you know ignorance doesn't lead to bliss.

Finally, it must be said that this book does not offer any financial advice, recommendations or solicitations and assumes no liability (of any kind) in any decisions (conscious or unintentional) made by you, dear reader. It's intended as a tongue-in-cheek introduction to finance and if, along the way, I offend anyone, please do not take it personally. So, come now with me for a journey to the land of *Moolah or Bummer!* I hope that by the end of the book you will be closer to choosing *Moolah*, not *Bummer!*, in your life.

401(K) RETIREMENT PLAN

With the big 40 around the corner
You're starting to feel a little skittish
about your retirement.
Waiting at a red light,
You see a homeless person.
You read the cardboard placard.
"Start investing now for retirement.
Don't end up like me."
The light changes to green.
As you accelerate away
You consider your options.
How about your company's 401(k) retirement plan?
They'll automatically deduct
from your paycheck,
before you can touch it.
The money that's invested isn't taxed
until you withdraw it at retirement.

Do you or don't you?
Will you or won't you?
Which will it be?
MOOLAH or BUMMER?

MOOLAH
Scared of being a bag lady,
you sign up for the plan.

You wisely select diversified investments and,
to top if off,
your company matches your contribution.

BUMMER!
Although you sign up for the 401(k) plan,
you allocate it all to company stock.
You loyal worker bee!
But the top dogs at your company "Enron" you,
fooling you all and running off with the loot.
Now your retirement account ain't worth a dime.
Bummer.

ASSET & LIABILITY

Drop dead gorgeous Anna saunters by,
But as they say, beauty is in the eye of the beholder.
What's an asset to some
is a liability to others.
Like your home.
Most homeowners believe their house
is their biggest asset,
because it's probably the most expensive item
they'll ever *own*.
But looking at it another way,
your home is also your biggest liability
because it's the biggest amount of money you *owe*.
You're deciding whether to own a home or not,
and wondering, "Would Anna
be an asset or a liability?"

Do you or don't you?
Will you or won't you?
Which will it be?
MOOLAH or BUMMER?

MOOLAH
Monthly mortgage payments
would eat up a big chunk of your income,
money that could instead
go toward other investment opportunities.
You strike a happy medium.
You purchase a modest yet comfortable home,
and put the remaining money
in other investments.
Your home is an asset.

BUMMER!
You like the idea of owning your own home,
but not just any house.

It's got to be a showpiece property,
just like the trophy girlfriend you seek.
You purchase the castle
but after paying the mega-sized mortgage every month,
you've little money over to do anything else.
Your house is a liability.
So is Anna.
Bummer.

BANKRUPTCY

You're a responsible person.
You hold down a steady job.
You pay your bills on time.
You even mentor da neighborhood kids.
If "da kids" only knew about your nasty little habit.
Some say it's gambling,
but to you online poker
is a game of skill.
You keep chasing higher stakes.
Bigger wins,
or bigger losses?

Do you or don't you?
Will you or won't you?
Which will it be?
MOOLAH or BUMMER?

MOOLAH
One midnight,
as you're placing bets,
the doorbell rings.
It's the pizza boy.
"Hey, Mr. Sam! How you doin?"
It's Tommy, one of "da kids".
You're unable to look Tommy in the eye
And stuff a bigger tip than usual in his shirt pocket.
But the pizza doesn't taste the same.
You quit playing poker
Da next day.

BUMMER!
When you don't
change out of your PJ's
you're addicted.
And you lose!

You lose SO BIG
you can't pay your debts
and have to declare bankruptcy.
Now, all you have are your Superhero PJ's.
Da kids think you're *some* Superhero.
Bummer.

BONDS

You're immersed in your favorite video game,
a Superhero in pursuit of twelve crazy monsters.
Having just captured the Cyber Monster of Garumba,
you're about to slaughter it mercilessly
when you're interrupted by Dick, your financial advisor.
Dick urges you to buy bonds.
"The stock market is over. Buy bonds!
Bonds are debt issued by institutions and governments.
When you buy bonds you lend them your moolah.
In return, you'll get interest payments
And when the bonds mature
you'll be repaid what you lent them."
Bonds? The only bond you know is James Bond,
that chivalrous agent from Her Majesty's Secret Service.
Do you slay the Cyber Monster of Garumba
or quit the game to buy bonds?

Do you or don't you?
Will you or won't you?
Which will it be?
MOOLAH or BUMMER?

MOOLAH
You quit the game to buy bonds
But not before a nanosecond jab
to the Cyber Monster's left flank.
Risk-averse, you choose
U.S. government and investment-grade bonds.
Your timing couldn't be better.
Later, when interest rates drop,
You're still paid the same interest as before.

BUMMER!
You quit the game.
Tempted by higher interest payments,

you choose speculative high yield bonds.
But they're also known as junk bonds,
and when the companies are
unable to fulfill their obligations
you're slaughtered on the pillars of greed!
Bummer.

BOUNCE

You're living from paycheck to paycheck,
barely making ends meet.
Then you see it, the latest video game system,
and you want it so badly.
3D touchscreen, wireless, multiple players!
Jump Mario, jump!
You take out your checkbook,
ready to sign your John Hancock,
hoping the check won't be cashed
before your paycheck arrives on Friday.

Do you or don't you?
Will you or won't you?
Which will it be?
MOOLAH or BUMMER?

MOOLAH
Waiting in line for the game gizmo,
what once seemed so essential
now appears so temporary.
As your yoga teacher says,
"Nothing lasting was ever created by man."
You hastily put away your checkbook,
And take a deep cleansing breath.

BUMMER!
Without further hesitation,
you sign your John Hancock.
But the check is deposited before your paycheck.
It bounces.
Boing, boing, boing.
The bank returns the check
and charges you $39 because of insufficient funds.
Bummer.

BULL MARKET

Yay! It's a BULL MARKET! Toro!
That means most stocks are up, up, up.
Maybe you'll take that big trip
to beautiful Pamplona, Spain
to see "the running of the bulls".
How poetic, since it's the bull market
that'll give you the money to go.
But bull market or not,
how will your portfolio do?

Do you or don't you?
Will you or won't you?
Which will it be?
MOOLAH or BUMMER?

MOOLAH
Yes, you invested in Index Funds
which track the market's performance.
Your stocks are up!
You're on your way
to celebrate the running of the bulls.
Toro!

BUMMER!
Nooo!
You remember that
you invested in Defensive Stocks,
and down they go,
just like past bull markets.
No Spain. No bulls.
That defensive advice
turned out to be a whole lotta bull.
Bummer.

CAPITAL GAINS

It's December and you're aching
for a golf vacation in Hawaii.
You're considering selling
the stocks you bought last January
to pay for the clubs.
But you realize that
by selling the stocks
before a year has passed,
your profits will get taxed
at your personal income rate
instead of at the lower capital gains rate.
Do you sell or hold?

Do you or don't you?
Will you or won't you?
Which will it be?
MOOLAH or BUMMER?

MOOLAH
Yes! You hold it a full year
and get taxed at the lower capital gains rate.
Enjoy Hawaii!
Hula, hula, hula!

BUMMER!
No! You don't have an accountant's mind.
You sell now and live vicariously.
You end up unable to pay the golf course fees.
Bummer.

COMPOUND INTEREST

Ever since you signed up
for a free internet dating service,
you've been receiving SPAM.
You feel it's nobody's business
whether your love life needs rejuvenating
and you've already got enough vitamins.
But those emails keep multiplying,
growing exponentially like compound interest.
Each email seems to spawn more email,
which just compounds the problem.
SPAM sucks!
If only your bank account would
multiply like a SPAM virus.

Do you or don't you?
Will you or won't you?
Which will it be?
MOOLAH or BUMMER?

MOOLAH
Yay! Your checking account
pays compound interest,
so you receive interest on the principal
(the amount you originally deposited)
as well as on the interest it earns!
Like your childhood hero, Bugs Bunny,
You love multiplication.

BUMMER!
Every time there's an interest payment
Your checking account pays *simple* interest.
No exponential growth for you.
Bummer.

COLLATERAL

You and your sweetie are about to become homeowners!
Aaah, the American dream…
a house in the suburbs with white picket fence,
a couple of RugRats and a golden retriever.
The loan officer asks for collateral,
valuable stuff the bank can take
if you default on the loan.
So you put up everything you own…
monster truck, heirloom clock,
wedding ring with mega rock.
"Now sign these papers," the loan officer says
And hands over a thousand pages give or take.

Do you or don't you?
Will you or won't you?
Which will it be?
MOOLAH or BUMMER?

MOOLAH
You sign the papers.
And all goes as expected.
You've got a house in the 'burbs with white picket fence,
a couple of RugRats and a golden retriever,
a monster truck, heirloom clock,
a wedding ring with mega rock.

BUMMER!
You sign the papers.
And all goes as expected
until the day you're downsized.
For a while, you scrape by
but your sweetie's income ain't enough
and your savings won't last forever.
You don't want to lose your house.
You sell the monster truck and heirloom clock,

But not the wedding ring with mega rock.
Bummer.

CONSUMER INTEREST

In the good ol' USA,
all interest is not equal.
Interest on your home
(the one you live in)
is tax deductible.
But consumer interest
(interest on consumer loans
for cars, stereos, pretty clothes),
well, you foot da whole bill.
As your eye caresses the curves
Of a beautiful red Corvette,
Only you can decide:
Hot wheels or home?

Do you or don't you?
Will you or won't you?
Which will it be?
MOOLAH or BUMMER?

MOOLAH
Commonsense wins
over the need for speed.
You Metro Mini suits you just fine.

BUMMER!
You're an adrenaline junkie.
As you zoom away
from the car dealership
You're thinking,
"Life is too short."
Bummer.

CONTRARIAN OPINION

"Candy is a saturated market",
you've been told a 1000 times before.
But you're a Contrarian.
You believe the market moves opposite
to most small investors' expectations.
You prefer to watch for "the signs."
Out at your local 24-hour convenience store one day,
you see a flock of ravenous kids
raiding the candy aisle.
It seems there's a gold mine in candy
if you watch the kids.
Because you're a contrarian
you invest in the company that makes
these sour-exploding-ultraviolet-nuclear jawbreakers.
Does your contrariness pay off?

Do you or don't you?
Will you or won't you?
Which will it be?
MOOLAH or BUMMER?

MOOLAH
Good instincts!
It turns out the jawbreakers are
the "Next Big Thing."
Your contrariness pays off.

BUMMER!
Tough luck.
The candy was popular
until kids' heads began glowing
an eerie green at night.
You'll be more agreeable in future.
Bummer.

CORPORATE ANNOUNCEMENT

Here's a press release from Info Gods Inc.
announcing the launch of
the Omnituitive series of laptops.
Investors are told these computers
will be self-aware, deviously intelligent
and frighteningly powerful.
Others interpret it
as a marketing ploy.
But you want to believe.
Do you buy some shares?

Do you or don't you?
Will you or won't you?
Which will it be?
MOOLAH or BUMMER?

MOOLAH
You buy, after doing due diligence.
The laptops live up to their unbelievable billing.
The shares surge.
You now have $6 big ones
and a computer named Spot.

BUMMER!
You buy,
but the announcements were empty.
Now, so is your wallet.
Bummer.

CREDIT CARD

You never realized
how desirable you are
until you started receiving all those
free credit cards in the mail.
Is it the tropical breeze deodorant,
or your extreme makeover
with the darling cheekbones?
Suddenly, you can have the bucks to support
the lifestyle you've always dreamed of.
Do you activate the credit cards?

Do you or don't you?
Will you or won't you?
Which will it be?
MOOLAH or BUMMER?

MOOLAH
You activate one credit card
and treat it wisely,
living within your means.
You pay off the entire balance every month,
Building up a history of good credit.

BUMMER!
You go wild,
spending like there's no tomorrow in sight.
You run up enormous credit card debt,
and can't afford to pay off the balance.
Now they're got you
paying super high interest payments.
Bummer.

DAYTRADERS

Bored with your job,
you quit to take up daytrading.
Over the course of the day
you buy and sell stocks many times.
You like the risks and rewards,
and the excitement you always wanted.
Will your career gamble pay off,
or will you be sending out your resume?

Do you or don't you?
Will you or won't you?
Which will it be?
MOOLAH or BUMMER?

MOOLAH
Whoo-hoo!!!
You turn out to be wildly skillful at it.
You cleanup and
buy the company you used to work for.
Take that, Boss!

BUMMER!
Uh oh.
You get more excitement than you counted on.
Like many daytraders,
You lose all your money.
It's resume time.
Bummer.

DEBT

You meet the coolest, sweetest person.
Now, you're in love with each other.
It's sheer bliss and passion!
You're starting to think maybe long term.
You want to share yourself completely.
Then you remember the huge debt you're in.
It started small
but is now a bad habit
that keeps growing and growing,
one eensy-weensy purchase at a time.
You don't even know how much you owe anymore.
Should you keep the debt a secret,
or listen to Dr. Phil and
"Tell it like it is".

Do you or don't you?
Will you or won't you?
Which will it be?
MOOLAH or BUMMER?

MOOLAH
You find the courage to reveal your debt.
Instead of leaving you
for someone fiscally responsible,
your sweetheart totally understands.
Her love is unconditional.
You pledge your love to each other.
You vow to cut your debt.

BUMMER!
You were honest with your last love.
It backfired.
So this time you keep the secret.
But one day, the truth comes out.
She dumps you, saying,

"You can't teach an old dog new tricks."
Bummer.

DIVIDENDS

You have a sailor's heart.
You're living off the grid
in a sailboat on the bay
going from port to port,
visiting friends like olden times.
But your source of income
is very modern indeed.
You live on dividend payouts
from investments in the stock market.
But lately, you feel some concern
about market stability.
Should you buy, sell or hold?

Do you or don't you?
Will you or won't you?
Which will it be?
MOOLAH or BUMMER?

MOOLAH
Bon Voyage!
The companies you invested in
continue their historical growth,
and dividend payouts
are both consistent and strong.

BUMMER!
The companies you invested in
veer off course,
charting unknown waters.
Dividends dry up.
You'll be staying in port.
Bummer.

DOW JONES INDUSTRIAL AVERAGE

At business school
you learned that Dow
is not only the name of a company
that makes mace and sandwich bags,
it's also another name for
the average price of 30 industrial stocks
chosen to represent how the overall market is doing.
Currently, the Dow is up for the year.
You're considering buying Index Funds
which track how the overall market is doing.

Do you or don't you?
Will you or won't you?
Which will it be?
MOOLAH or BUMMER?

MOOLAH
You buy.
The Dow continues up!
Confidence is high
and so are your stocks.

BUMMER!
You buy.
The Dow loses steam.
Because you can't afford
fancy lunches anymore,
You buy more sandwich bags.
Good ol' PB & J!
Bummer.

DOWNPAYMENT

You just got a big promotion!
Big title. Power. Serious money.
Already, Dilbert irritates you
and Trump is *the* man.
Finally, you'll be able to afford a house.
But what to do about the downpayment,
usually about 20% of the home price?
You'd feel guilty asking your parents,
and you feel qualmish
about the risky mortgages being touted
by some smooth-talking salespeople.
You wish you could turn back time
and have saved more.

Do you or don't you?
Will you or won't you?
Which will it be?
MOOLAH or BUMMER?

MOOLAH
Remembering those pre-Viagra days
and how they struggled financially,
your mom and dad
offer you a bridge loan
to help you temporarily.
You're so thankful
you immediately start schmoozing
for your next promotion.
And you pay your folks back a little with every paycheck.

BUMMER!
Feeling caught between a rock and a hard place,
you go for a risky mortgage.
It's a gamble
but there's no downpayment required.

Everyday you're sweating bullets
that interest rates won't rise.
You're not sure the angst is worth it.
You start Viagra prematurely.
Bummer.

EARNINGS EXPECTATIONS

Online Auctions Galore (OAG),
a company you invested in years ago,
reports they expect to earn
less than expected this quarter.
People you know begin to sell the stock
to invest in something else
with better earnings expectations.
But you want to keep the stock
for sentimental reasons.

Do you or don't you?
Will you or won't you?
Which will it be?
MOOLAH or BUMMER?

MOOLAH
And it's a good thing you kept the stock.
OAG gave a conservative estimate
and comes in ahead of expectations.

BUMMER!
Your buddies were right.
The company is dysfunctional
and misses their earnings expectations.
To make matters worse,
the company fudged their books
to hide how bad the results really are.
Bummer.

EVENT RISK

Due to new discoveries in ESP,
people worldwide
are giving up their cell phones
and wireless connections
for intuitive, mind-to-mind communication.
Pretty cool, huh!
There is no way you could have
possibly predicted this event.
How do the markets react
to this liberating development?

Do you or don't you?
Will you or won't you?
Which will it be?
MOOLAH or BUMMER?

MOOLAH
Luckily, you never
owned telecom stock.
So, the ESP thing
works out pretty well for you.

BUMMER!
Unfortunately, you were
heavily invested in telecom stocks.
So the ESP thing
kills your finances.
You wish you could have predicted this event.
But that's a risk of investing.
Bummer.

FICO

At the Aussie Bar 'n Grill,
Rob and Jeff are hanging out.
"4", grunts Rob
as an attractive lady sashays by.
"7", counters Jeff.
Across the room, you and Dave
are doing a little scoring of your own.
"Uh-oh, looks like an 800 just walked in",
moans Dave in his Neanderthal way.
Puzzled, the bartender asks,
"Is that a new scoring system?"
So you explain, "We're talking FICO scores.
You know, a person's credit rating.
Above 760 is a real catch."
Then Dave turns to you,
"Wanna go for it?"

Do you or don't you?
Will you or won't you?
Which will it be?
MOOLAH or BUMMER?

MOOLAH
You go for it.
And she's a winner.
As much as you try to uncover
skeletons in her closet,
Samantha's credit history is squeeky clean.

BUMMER!
Looks can be deceiving.
Samantha's designer clothes
and flashy European convertible
were purchased on credit,
and the balance is long overdue.

It shows in her low FICO score.
Too bad!
Ugga, ugga, ugga.

FIXED & ADJUSTABLE MORTGAGE RATE

You're not old enough to have lived
through the Great Depression,
but Grandpappy doesn't let you forget
how your family survived on beans.
Baked beans, bean soup,
bean casserole, bean cakes...
beans, beans, beans.
Now you're purchasing your first house
and the loan officer asks whether you want
a fixed or adjustable rate mortgage (ARM).
Visions of refried beans waft above her head
like a Diego Cuevara painting.
Sure, the mortgage rate
(the interest rate on a home loan)
is lower for the adjustable than the fixed,
but the ARM can shoot up
if interest rates rise.

Do you or don't you?
Will you or won't you?
Which will it be?
MOOLAH or BUMMER?

MOOLAH
Sure the ARM is lower
But you choose the fixed rate,
because you'll know *exactly*
how much you'll owe
for the life of the loan.

BUMMER!
You choose the ARM.
All goes well until interest rates rise.
Now you have to pay escalating rates.

As you eat your chilli,
You wonder when the end will be in sight.
Bummer.

FORECLOSURE

Tired of being a renter,
you're working as hard as you can
to afford a house.
Being at the office routinely until 10pm,
you don't have time to cook.
That's okay, you order take-out.
Chicken burritos, moo shu pork...
you love all the flavors of the world.
Back at your apartment
you dig in while watching the food channel.
Well, choosing which house to buy
is a little like selecting dinner.
There are so many choices.

Do you or don't you?
Will you or won't you?
Which will it be?
MOOLAH or BUMMER?

MOOLAH
Although you enjoy watching the food divas,
your favorite dish is mom's spaghetti and meatballs.
The house you purchase is charming and affordable.
There's even enough left over for dessert.

BUMMER!
The house you select is like
foie gras and duck confit;
terrific choices,
but you bit off more than you can chew.
Now you're unable to make the mortgage payments.
The bank forecloses the house,
repossessing it and putting it up for sale
to cover the outstanding debt.
Back in your apartment

You're eating tuna casserole
with hamburger helper.
Bummer.

FUNDAMENTAL ANALYSIS

Bored of your rugged lifestyle
as a New Zealand sheepherder,
You decide to pour hours of time
into analyzing a company's financial statements,
competitive position and industry.
You see an angle,
sell some sheep
and buy some shares.
Will your fundamental analysis reward you?
Or is stock picking like the lottery?

Do you or don't you?
Will you or won't you?
Which will it be?
MOOLAH or BUMMER?

MOOLAH
You're a solid analyst.
You retire from the shepherd's life
to race Ferraris on the Corsican Grand Prix.

BUMMER!
You're no better an analyst than your sheep.
You're better off with your knitting group
than analyzing.
Bummer.

GROSS DOMESTIC PRODUCT

GDP is the Big Kahuna
of measuring the health
of the economy.
When it's up, the nation is
creating a lot of "stuff",
and people feel confident
in the economy.
During the "Go-Go 80's"
the GDP was robust
and people felt invincible.
So how is GDP doing now?

Do you or don't you?
Will you or won't you?
Which will it be?
MOOLAH or BUMMER?

MOOLAH
The economy is
humming along right now,
and people feel
optimistic enough to invest.
Your portfolio is rising
along with the GDP.

BUMMER!
Now the GDP is down.
People feel vulnerable,
so they shy away from spending and investing,
Your portfolio drops with the GDP.
Bummer.

HOMEOWNER'S EQUITY (1)

To some, home ownership is like surfing
progressively bigger waves.
After gentle Malibu they move on
to Tressles and Santa Cruz
and ultimately, Pipeline.
When their house appreciates in value,
they sell it and use their increased equity
to purchase the next house.
It's usually bigger and pricier.
Paddling out in the aquamarine waters one day,
watching the clouds across the azure sky,
waiting to catch the next wave,
you consider the current market price of your home
and whether to make the next move up.

Do you or don't you?
Will you or won't you?
Which will it be?
MOOLAH or BUMMER

MOOLAH
The real estate market is enjoying
its share of irrational exuberance.
That's great for you,
because your home has doubled in value.
You sell and roll the increased equity
into a mini mansion.
Ride the wave!

BUMMER!
Yeah, everyone keeps moving up,
and you do too.
You sell your home
and because it doubled in value,
the increased equity qualifies you for a mini mansion.

But your new mortgage is almost
triple your previous one,
and when the bubble bursts,
you owe more than what you could sell the house for.
Bummer.

HOMEOWNER'S EQUITY (2)

The little fixer-upper
you were barely able to afford seven years ago
has sure risen in value.
You get an endorphin high
just watching your home price run up.
Friends who rent trendy downtown lofts
envy you.
It may be small but at least you're in the market.
Enrico, your pilates trainer, suggests you
take out some of the increase in equity
to have some fun.

Do you or don't you?
Will you or won't you?
Which will it be?
MOOLAH or BUMMER?

MOOLAH
You follow Enrico's advice.
You borrow from the equity
you have in your house
to pay off your credit card debt.
You come out ahead
because your mortgage rate
is a lot lower than your credit card interest rate.

BUMMER!
You follow Enrico's advice literally.
You go on a shopping spree,
truly believing you've got moolah to burn.
But although your home is worth more,
your increased wealth is all "on paper".
And since you bought more stuff,
you now have greater debt,

greater real debt.
Bummer.

IMPORTANCE OF DIVERSIFICATION

You're friends with Jerry Jay
who started his own tech company.
You love your buddy and the technology,
so you consider selling your entire diverse portfolio
to help finance this new, wild, potentially great company.
Jerry promises you a seat on the board of directors.

Do you or don't you?
Will you or won't you?
Which will it be?
MOOLAH or BUMMER?

MOOLAH
You join Jerry Jay on his wild adventure.
The two of you grow the company.
Your single mindedness pays off.

BUMMER!
You sell your portfolio to finance Jerry's company,
but he's a better friend than businessman.
Your one and only investment sinks with you "on board".
You shoulda stayed diversified.
Bummer.

INCOME PROPERTY

After the zoom-zoom of the nineties,
your portfolio crashed and burned in the stock market.
You dumped the once sexy tech stocks,
seeing them as a bunch of smoke and mirrors.
Using advanced GPS,
you chart a new course for your portfolio,
redirecting it away from stocks
and instead towards real estate.
Your radar turns to apartment rentals.
The rents collected would fuel your cash flow.

Do you or don't you?
Will you or won't you?
Which will it be?
MOOLAH or BUMMER?

MOOLAH
You follow through with the course you charted,
hiring a property manager
to collect the rents and manage the apartments.
The commission is a small price to pay.
The rents cover the mortgage
and the property appreciation
builds nice equity for you.

BUMMER!
Just before the rents are due
every month, around 3am,
you get the phone calls…
The toilets are clogged
with mysterious objects.
Being a landlord sucks!
Bummer.

INFLATION

You're a basic kind of guy,
with very basic needs.
Your refrigerator usually contains three items:
light, dark and draft.
Because you consume so little,
you feel pretty immune to inflation,
the rate at which prices for services and stuff is rising.
Even your investments
are managed in a very basic way.
You always keep cash for basic living expenses,
and you put the rest in a savings account.
Just recently your girlfriend warned you of inflation risk,
the risk that the return on your investments
will be negative after adjusting for inflation.
Do you move your savings or stay put?

Do you or don't you?
Will you or won't you?
Which will it be?
MOOLAH or BUMMER?

MOOLAH
Alas, with the stock market down
and bonds in a limbo,
with interest rates low
and real estate sky high,
there ain't too many alternatives.
So you do the next best thing for you.
You use your savings to pay off your credit card debt!
And the credit card interest you save is
like getting a return on your money!

BUMMER!
You stay put.
Since your savings account pays 2% interest

it barely keeps pace with inflation.
With such a low return you may as well
stick your money in a shoebox.
Bummer.

INTEREST

If the 60's were about free love,
then some would have you believe
today is about free money.
Well, almost.
"Interest" gets you access
to money you don't have.
Interest is the price paid for borrowing money,
expressed as a percentage rate
over a period of time (e.g. 7% per year).
No longer content with love beads,
And "love, love, love me do",
today's consumer loads ups on
refrigerators, power tools and SUV's.
How about you?

Do you or don't you?
Will you or won't you?
Which will it be?
MOOLAH or BUMMER?

MOOLAH
You were never into fads,
whether free love or easy money.
You have enough real love in your life
and you don't need a loan for more
stuff you don't want.

BUMMER!
Perhaps you should have stuck
with the "love, love, love me do".
Now you're $17,000 in the hole
plus the interest you owe.
Bummer.

*(At a 7% interest rate, you owe an extra $1,190
which is the interest on $17,000).*

IDENTITY THEFT

You're John Edward Doe.
Born Long Island, 1971 to John and Dottie Doe.
Second child of three.
Graduated Morse High School,
"Most unlikely to succeed".
By day, you're a loyal cubicle drone.
By night, after many jugs of java,
your keyboard strokes teeter-totter
between honorable intentions
and finding your true love.
So late one night,
way past the legal caffeine limit,
you sign up to meet your ideal mate.
You answer 20 questions and then,
most important, enter your credit card number.
All that remains is to press "Submit".
But what about all those identity theft horror stories?

Do you or don't you?
Will you or won't you?
Which will it be?
MOOLAH or BUMMER?

MOOLAH
It's a secure site.
Encrypted.
Password protected.
Virus free.
Nothing unremarkable happened except, wait!
You meet the love of your life!

BUMMER!
Sorry, you're out of luck!
They stole your identity
and took you all the way to the cleaners.

Your bank account has been depleted,
you've got credit card bills up the yin yang,
and it'll cost about $20K
to restore your identity.
Now you know it pays to be paranoid.
Bummer.

INDUSTRIAL PRODUCTION

Today at the local auto cross circuit,
you and some other gents in the pits
lament about how fewer cars are being made this year.
The monthly industrial production figures have dropped.
To investors, this is a sign the economy is slowing down.
Everyone in the pits is bummed 'cos this
could increase the cost of mods, wheels
and tweakable fuel injection microchips.
How reliable are economic indicators?
Isn't there opportunity in both good and bad times?

Do you or don't you?
Will you or won't you?
Which will it be?
MOOLAH or BUMMER?

MOOLAH
It turns out that baby boomers
want to continue driving around
during their mid life crisis
so industrial production remains powerful.
You thank your buddies with receding hairlines.

BUMMER!
Demand for tweakable fuel injection microchips slows
and mirrors the downtrend in industrial production.
Investors stay on the sidelines,
having little reason to rally.
Bummer.

INSIDER TRADING

Your back is sore, your throat is dry.
You're stuffed into a chair
going 600 mph, 35,000 feet in the air.
You're on a flight from San Francisco to Boston
for a job you hate.
On the very same flight,
you hear your company's
two quantum-virus-chip engineers talking.
You hear then discussing a new 8 nanometer,
multi-DNA, reverse-spin super-chip.
It will be announced to the media in just three days.
You know insider trading is illegal,
but it's soooo tempting.

Do you or don't you?
Will you or won't you?
Which will it be?
MOOLAH or BUMMER?

MOOLAH
You resist the urge to slime yourself.
Mom 'n Dad and your kindergarten teacher
would be proud of you.

BUMMER!
You buy heavily.
Four days later you're driving
your new Luxo-car around town
when you get a call from the Feds.
Five days later you're squealing like a pig
in a Full Nelson to avoid going to jail.
Six days later,
having avoided a cellmate named "Smiling Guido",
you're on another flight to Boston for your old job.

And now, it doesn't seem so bad.
Bummer.

INTERNET CHAT ROOMS

You're in an internet chat room
with "heidi 21xxx".
You've chatted for months now
and you're falling for her.
You share a mutual interest.
She seems to know investing well,
so you take her advice and invest some.
Will Heidi's advice bring you newfound wealth?

Do you or don't you?
Will you or won't you?
Which will it be?
MOOLAH or BUMMER?

MOOLAH
The tips were spectacular,
and so is Heidi when you meet her in real life.
The wedding is in May.

BUMMER!
"heidi 25xxx" turns out to be
a dirty old man.
And the tips were no better.
Bummer.

INVESTMENT CHOICES

Boyfriends are like investment choices…
there are all kinds out there.
Norm is like a T-Bill…
safe, guaranteed and predictable
but with a small return.
Marco is sexy and tempestuous
with a biotech stock's mystique
and the allure of a spectacular future.
Axel is like a junk bond…
high risk and exciting
Chuck, he's prime real estate.
Matt is schizophrenic
like a nicely diversified portfolio.
Who do you choose
and how will you do?

Do you or don't you?
Will you or won't you?
Which will it be?
MOOLAH or BUMMER?

MOOLAH
You chose Matt.
His multiple personalities entertain you,
and he does all right
through good and bad.
You win at love and money!

BUMMER!
You chose Marco,
putting your hopes in his promise
of a spectacular future.
So you wait for the next cure for cancer,
And you wait and you wait and you wait.
Bummer.

INDIVIDUAL TAX RETURN

Remember your first paycheck?
You felt so proud you almost framed it.
Now remember that little section
on your pay stub where taxes are deducted?
After taxes, you ended up with
about half of your salary.
That $4 super high octane bull juice
really costs about $8 in pre-tax money.
That $350 surfboard is really gonna cost
about $700 of pre-tax income!
Wow, you're gonna really want to
chase some big kahunas at that price.
Even choosing between regular and large fries
is a more momentous decision
when one considers the tax effect.

Do you or don't you?
Will you or won't you?
Which will it be?
MOOLAH or BUMMER?

MOOLAH
Reality is great!
You overrestimated your tax deductions.
You have to send Uncle Sam a check
to cover the difference next April 15.
That's okay! You owed that money anyway.
Meanwhile, you invested the difference
and earned a modest return,
enough for a new surfboard!

BUMMER!
Reality sucks!
You're paying so much in taxes
you don't have enough over for a new surfboard.

Your decision making stays at
regular or super size fries.
Bummer.

INTEREST RATES

Normally, you're very interested in
what "the Fed" has to say about interest rates.
When market watchers hear rates are going to drop,
money usually flows into the market.
Right now it's hard to say which way the Fed will go,
but experts are predicting rates will drop.

Do you or don't you?
Will you or won't you?
Which will it be?
MOOLAH or BUMMER?

MOOLAH
Surprise!
The Fed approves an even bigger rate drop
than expected
to stimulate our sluggish economy.
A stock rally ensues,
lifting your portfolio value
and making for a madhouse
on the trading floor.
So what if coffee gets spilled
on your favorite blue Gabardine suit?

BUMMER!
The pro's were fooled!
And so were you!
The Fed does nothing
and no stock rally follows.
Bummer.

INVESTMENT CLUB

Out dancing one night,
you and your honey
meet a group of
like minded people
who want to start
an investment club.
And so it is,
in the wee hours of a frosty morning,
that The Ocean Air Tango & Investment Club
is born.
The twelve of you
research stocks,
vote on potential investments,
do the tango,
and pool your resources
to buy shares.
Is it true the more the merrier?

Do you or don't you?
Will you or won't you?
Which will it be?
MOOLAH or BUMMER?

MOOLAH
One year later,
the Ocean Air Tango & Investment Club is $57K richer,
and you and your fellow investors
have become true friends.
Cha, cha, cha!
kaChing. kaChing.

BUMMER!
One year later,
your club is $22K poorer.
You club dissolves.

You blame everyone
but yourself.
You switch to dancing with yourself.
Bummer.

LATE CHARGE

Your "buds" describe you as laid back,
and you take it as a compliment.
But when your monthly loan statement arrives
with a $39 "late fee" you're not too amused.
You know it's the rebel in you
that causes you to send the check late,
but you're not sure you're ready to grow up yet.
Then again, $39 can buy
a lot of liquid refreshment,
diet cola and vitamin water of course.
Do you start paying your bills on time?

Do you or don't you?
Will you or won't you?
Which will it be?
MOOLAH or BUMMER?

MOOLAH
All those lazy little slip-ups
could already have bought you
a nice getaway weekend.
You reckon it's finally time to grow up.

BUMMER!
You'd rather be a disorganized slouch
than have to clean up your home office
and balance your checkbook.
But it's not that simple…
your credit score will fall
if you continue your slothful ways.
Then, should you apply for a loan
you'll be charged a higher interest rate.
When you live for today,
You'll pay the price tomorrow.
Bummer.

LIFE INSURANCE

Nowadays, there's too much reality on TV.
Well, you've been coping with some reality yourself.
You haven't had to eat bulls' testicles,
but your spouse was the unlucky victim
in some illicit streetcar racing.
It's true some of your spouse's habits
grated on your nerves,
like the nose-picking
(okay at home, just not in public),
but you still loved him.
Now what do you do?

Do you or don't you?
Will you or won't you?
Which will it be?
MOOLAH or BUMMER?

MOOLAH
The answer is term life insurance,
which both of you enrolled in.

BUMMER!
Your heart is grieving and,
since your spouse didn't have a life insurance policy,
your kids will be wearing Thrift
instead of designer clothes.
Bummer.

I.P.O.
Initial Public Offering

During the Dot-com hoopla
many Internet companies tripled in value
at their initial public offering of stock.
Investors blindly fed massive amounts of money
into companies they didn't understand,
but hoped would make them rich.
How about you?
Were you a casualty
or one of the lucky few?

Do you or don't you?
Will you or won't you?
Which will it be?
MOOLAH or BUMMER?

MOOLAH
Luckily, you made your money
then got out
before the other investors wizened up.

BUMMER!
Unfortunately, you were another
greedy, inexperienced moth
caught in the IPO flame.
Bummer.

LIFETIME REVERSE MORTGAGE

Your spouse is the worrying kind.
Mostly he worries about running out of something.
His top 10 list includes: hot sauce,
deodorant, toilet paper, beer and
of course clean underwear.
Now that both of you are getting older,
his favorite worry is running out of retirement funds.
"You can't count on social security", he says.
"In the spirit of the lone ranger riding West,
we're going to have to do it ourselves."
But with only your house as your main investment,
and the clock ticking, what do you do?

Do you or don't you?
Will you or won't you?
Which will it be?
MOOLAH or BUMMER?

MOOLAH
The answer is a lifetime reverse mortgage.
It lets homeowners borrow
against the value of their home,
while retaining title,
and making no payments while still living there.
Yee-haw!

BUMMER!
With a lifetime reverse mortgage
when you pass away the property may be sold
so the loan can be repaid.
Bummer for your heirs.

LIMIT ORDERS

You want to improve your lifestyle.
You begin yoga and "Buy Organic".
You even make a decision to sell off your stocks
in "Happy Burger International".
You put in a limit order for $19.
This means the lowest price you will sell
each share for is $19.
Then Mad Cow Disease is found on a small ranch.
Oh no, will your limit order go through in time?

Do you or don't you?
Will you or won't you?
Which will it be?
MOOLAH or BUMMER?

MOOLAH
Fortunately your limit order
went through before the price got below $19.
So you're out of the meat business
and profitable too!

BUMMER!
Oh no! The sale of your stock
didn't happen before the price dropped.
Now, you're stuck with 300 shares
of a worthless stock
you don't even believe in.
Bummer.

MARGIN ACCOUNT

A new music technology called "Margarine Gold"
hits the streets and changes
how entertainment is experienced.
You like it so much you buy on margin,
borrowing money to afford the shares.
You're groovin' to the sound
of money you expect to be getting.
Will the risk you're taking
by buying on margin pay off?

Do you or don't you?
Will you or won't you?
Which will it be?
MOOLAH or BUMMER?

MOOLAH
Yay for "Margarine Gold!"
Spread it on everything!

BUMMER!
The stock price drops.
You receive a margin call you can't cover.
You're desperate,
and now you owe more
than you can sell the stock for.
What a meltdown!
Bummer.

MARKET BREADTH

Market breadth is measured by
the number of stocks that went up in price
versus those that went down.
Easy enough.
Today, Ambercroombie, a market analyst,
tells you, "Four hundred ninety-eight stocks went up in price."
Ditch, another analyst says,
"Three stocks went down in price today."
Putting two and two together,
your face forms a smile.
The market is going strong.
Do you sell to take the profits?

Do you or don't you?
Will you or won't you?
Which will it be?
MOOLAH or BUMMER?

MOOLAH
Oh yeah! You sell!
How you love those technical analysts.

BUMMER!
Oh no.
You remember you're invested
mainly in the NASDAQ
which fell.
Bummer.

MARKET CAPITALIZATION

A company's "market cap" is its stock price
multiplied by the number of its outstanding shares.
So, one company with many inexpensive stocks
can have the same market cap as another company
with very few pricey shares.
It's sorta like having many casual friends
versus having a few really good ones.
How will the companies you invest in do?
Will their market caps rise or drop?

Do you or don't you?
Will you or won't you?
Which will it be?
MOOLAH or BUMMER?

MOOLAH
Your market cap doubled
when the market price of your stocks doubled.
Throw your friends a party!

BUMMER!
Your market cap dropped
when your stock price dropped.
You obsess about it
and end up losing your casual friends.
Bummer.

MARKET ORDERS

Its chaos!
The market is up and down all day long
and you're getting nervous.
So on an "up" moment,
you put in a "market order"
to buy at $22 a share.
But with a "market order"
you don't pay the stock price
of when you placed the order,
you pay the price of the stock
when the order is executed.
What execution price do you get?

Do you or don't you?
Will you or won't you?
Which will it be?
MOOLAH or BUMMER?

MOOLAH
Wow! Lucky you!
The stock dropped to $20 a share
by the time your "market order" went through.
You paid $2 less per share!

BUMMER!
By the time your "market order"
went through the stock had risen to $24.
You paid $2 more for every share.
Bummer.

MARKET RISK

For Spring Break,
you vacation in beautiful Banana Beach.
To write it off as a business trip
you also visit an industrial factory
you bought shares in.
The trip begins splendidly
and the local seafood and tropical fruits are delicious.
But during your tour of the factory
the Independent Guerilla Front
kidnaps the company's administrators
and sets off incendiaries around underground fuel tanks.
You barely escape with your life.
You learn real life is risky.
So are the markets!
Will your investment survive
or become a bad vacation memory?

Do you or don't you?
Will you or won't you?
Which will it be?
MOOLAH or BUMMER?

MOOLAH
Luckily, the government intervenes.
Using strong-arm tactics
they restore stability and investor confidence.

BUMMER!
Unfortunately,
the situation goes from bad to worse.
All seven administrators perish.
The stock tanks.
Bummer.

MARKET UNCERTAINTY

You know how you never know
how a woman will feel
when you ask her out?
You know how sometimes
you can't really be sure
why men do what they do?
You know how you can't really
predict the weather?
Well friend,
this is the same kind of uncertainty
that exists in the stock market.
And right now, uncertainty in the market
is making investors sit on the sidelines.
How about you?

Do you or don't you?
Will you or won't you?
Which will it be?
MOOLAH or BUMMER?

MOOLAH
People and markets aren't certain,
but the Blue Chip stocks you invested in
continue their strong returns.

BUMMER!
The markets are uncertain,
and so are your nerves.
What seemed so surely "the next big thing"
has deflated like a bunch of hot air.
Bummer.

MARRIAGE PENALTY

Falling in love
happened accidentally.
Sure you've been infatuated countless times,
but always in a temporary way.
And then you met Jack
in the light bulb section
of the home improvement store.
The lights have been flashing ever since,
all the way to his marriage proposal.
But wait, before you tie the knot
you meet with Dick, your financial adviser.
"There's strength in numbers,"
he sagely espouses, "but also consider this…
a couple pays more tax
when filing jointly than they would
if they file individual tax returns."

Do you or don't you?
Will you or won't you?
Which will it be?
MOOLAH or BUMMER?

MOOLAH
You express your concerns to Jack.
He asks you to meet with *his* financial advisor, Lucy,
who shows you legitimate ways
to reduce your taxes,
offsetting the marriage penalty.
Now it's an easy decision.
You're getting married to Jack,
and for *all the right reasons.*

BUMMER!
You love Jack,

but you love your balance sheet even more.
Bummer.

MINIMUM PURCHASE

They're always telling you to save
for a golden sunset.
And being the pleasing kind,
you decide to follow through.
You figure after paying living expenses
you can invest $200 each month
and still maintain your lifestyle.
You evaluate your investment options.
Real estate? Nah, you don't have that amount of capital yet.
Anyway, isn't this the top of the market?
Forget the stock market.
It's way too risky.
How about a well diversified mutual fund
managed by a professional money manager
with a track record of steady growth?

Do you or don't you?
Will you or won't you?
Which will it be?
MOOLAH or BUMMER?

MOOLAH
Your good intentions *almost* come to a halt
when you learn of the mutual fund's
minimum purchase amount.
That's the minimum amount required
to open a new account.
Not to be outdone, you deposit $200 every month
in a money market account as a temporary investment.
It's FDIC insured up to $100,000, and liquid,
and helps you stick to your plan.
Then, when you've accumulated
the minimum purchase amount,
you move your savings to the mutual fund.
Life doesn't disappoint.

BUMMER!
Your good intentions come to a halt
when you learn of the mutual fund's
minimum purchase amount.
Who are they kidding?
Don't they want new business?
Bummer.

MONEY MARKET ACCOUNT

You used to get your thrills
from actively trading stocks.
It didn't really matter what you invested in.
You won as long as you got in 'n out in time.
Then the stock market bubble burst.
You lost so badly, you're scared of stocks now,
and you're seriously contemplating
parking your moolah in a money market account.
Small as it is,
you'd get a fixed return.
For sure.
Meanwhile, you could satisfy
your trading habit on Ebay.

Do you or don't you?
Will you or won't you?
Which will it be?
MOOLAH or BUMMER?

MOOLAH
For a while,
You receive the paltry but guaranteed interest payments.
Since the money market account is liquid,
you move your money without penalty
when better opportunities arise.

BUMMER!
You were burned so badly when the bubble burst,
you enter a state of investment paralysis,
staying in the money market waaay too long.
With interest rates at their lowest in years,
you're barely covering inflation.
Bummer.

MONEY SUPPLY

You love getting coffee and scones,
and you let no one get in your way.
However, the economy may be growing too rapidly,
which could lead to inflation,
rising interest rates
and a significant increase in the cost of butter.
Your sweet tooth recoils in horror
as every creamy, butter filled, French pastry
seems to have tripled in price.
Do you pay up?
You know you're worth it.

Do you or don't you?
Will you or won't you?
Which will it be?
MOOLAH or BUMMER?

MOOLAH
The economy later cools
and the money supply fattens up.
Aah, luscious French pastries!

BUMMER!
Your sweet tooth has a cavity.
You're paying too high a price
as inflation and rising interest rates
eat your finances for lunch.
You switch to donuts.
Bummer.

MORTGAGE RATE

The way real estate's been cruising,
you and your partner have been itching
to buy a place of your own.
Since the stock market tanked,
your mom's advice to get into real estate
is starting to make sense,
although you wonder if
you've already missed the boat.
Since you'll always need a roof over your heads,
you and your partner start looking at properties anyway.
Depending on which way mortgage rates go,
a fixer-upper house may be within your reach.
Which way do mortgage rates go?

Do you or don't you?
Will you or won't you?
Which will it be?
MOOLAH or BUMMER?

MOOLAH
To keep stimulating the economy,
the Fed drops interest rates by half a point.
There's a ripple effect to mortgage rates
which are at a record 40 year low!
Now you can definitely afford that house!
You can already smell the freshly cut grass
and the burgers on the barbie! Yeah!

BUMMER!
Aw shucks!
The Fed decides to raise interest rates
and there's a ripple effect to mortgage rates.
The higher rates will mean higher monthly payments.
You may have to settle for a condo.
Bummer.

MUTUAL FUND

They said to leave it to the professionals,
and you do. You invest in mutual funds.
Diversification and professional money management. Yeah!
And since you choose a no-load fund,
there's no commission!
Now you might just sit back
and let the professionals do their business
while you watch the latest Bart Simpson rerun.
How will the mutual fund do?

Do you or don't you?
Will you or won't you?
Which will it be?
MOOLAH or BUMMER?

MOOLAH
Hey, what do you know,
the experts really are experts!
You mutual fund has gained double digit growth.

BUMMER!
Yeah right, the mutual fund lags the S&P 500,
an index of 500 widely held common stocks
that measures the general performance of the market.
You realize the experts know
as much about investing as you do.
Bummer.

NASDAQ

The NASDAQ stock exchange
specializes in technology stocks,
and matches orders electronically.
This feature allows you to live in Rio
and work part time as a Copacabana lifeguard.
During a rescue at Barra Beach,
You're too busy to hear you beeping Palm.
It's your panicky stockbroker
telling you the NASDAQ is dropping.
Do you buy, sell or hold?

Do you or don't you?
Will you or won't you?
Which will it be?
MOOLAH or BUMMER?

MOOLAH
Your PDA says
your stocks are doing just fine,
as fine as the person you resuscitated on the beach.
You hold.

BUMMER!
The NASDAQ and your tech stocks
are taking a dive today.
You get back to your broker, but it's too late.
Your beach rescue is successful
but your stocks are drowning.
Bummer.

NYSE

Deep in the heart
of the concrete jungle of New York
lies the New York Stock Exchange.
Inside, piranha-like traders aggressively consume
any stocks that smell good.
As frenzied traders bite anything
that smells delicious
the excitement in the stock auction intensifies.
It's another beautiful day,
and blood is in the water.
Today, will you eat or be eaten?

Do you or don't you?
Will you or won't you?
Which will it be?
MOOLAH or BUMMER?

MOOLAH
Today, the blood in the water
belongs to someone else.
A whole school of tasty stocks
fell into the trading pool of the NYSE,
but not yours.

BUMMER!
Today, the blood in the water
is your own.
You get bitten by
bad stock purchases.
Get out of the deep!
Bummer.

OCTOBER 19, 1987 (BLACK MONDAY)

"…a date, which will live, in infamy!"
Four of the darkest days
in the stock market's history
occurred in October,
including "Black Monday."
Many people lost their savings
and became superstitiously fearful of this day.
But not you.

Do you or don't you?
Will you or won't you?
Which will it be?
MOOLAH or BUMMER?

MOOLAH
There's no need to fear this date.
It's just another day.
But others sell out of fear,
and you,
taking advantage
of their frayed nerves,
clean up.

BUMMER!
Fearing another crash like October 1987,
investors pull money out of the market.
Stocks plunge.
Your bravado is short-lived.
You develop a new respect
for "Black Monday".
Bummer.

OPEN/CLOSE PRICE

Another morning.
Get up, shower, eat
and still you aren't awake.
While waiting for your daily brew,
you check your stocks of
International Pharmaceutical Corporation.
The opening price is high
as the investment community
embraces its new wonder drug, "Pleasurex".
Pleased with your investment savvy
you head off to work.
Eight hours later,
you come home exhausted
and check IPC's closing price.
How did IPC do?

Do you or don't you?
Will you or won't you?
Which will it be?
MOOLAH or BUMMER?

MOOLAH
Demand for "Pleasurex" outstrips supply.
IPC's closing price
is 25% higher!
How sweet it is!

BUMMER!
IPC's closing price is down 25%
due to discoveries that "Pleasurex" is addictive.
The FDA requests additional data on the drug,
putting the party on hold.
"Damn those addicts," you say.
Bummer.

OPTIONS

Always having experienced difficulty committing,
you find yourself in a familiar situation.
This time it reminds you of Brad.
There were so many good things about him:
strong earnings, solid track record,
great growth potential, low debt to asset ratio…
So as you evaluate the Essential Lubricants Company,
you wonder whether
you'll regret passing up
the opportunity to invest.

Do you or don't you?
Will you or won't you?
Which will it be?
MOOLAH or BUMMER?

MOOLAH
Dick, your financial advisor suggests "options"
as a solution to your quandary.
"An option gives you the right,
but not the obligation,
to buy (or sell) the asset
at a set price
on or before a given date,
usually for a nominal cost".
Hey, your stomach can handle that!
So you buy options for ELC
and, true to history,
it keeps producing more and more essential lubricants.
You exercise your options and cash in!

BUMMER!
Global demand for essential lubricants
is growing at an eye-popping pace.
Brazil, China, Germany…can't get enough of the stuff.

But you decline the opportunity.
Your tummy can't handle the unknown.
So when ELC's market price triples,
all you can say is,
"Why didn't I learn from Brad?"
Bummer.

PAPER LOSSES

It's September
and your portfolio has plummeted,
but you're not worried.
Although September is historically
the worst month for stocks,
you're pretty confident these are just paper losses,
and in January, the money
will flow back into the market as usual.
Do you sell now and take the hit?
Or do you hold your paper losses
and hope the market picks up in January?

Do you or don't you?
Will you or won't you?
Which will it be?
MOOLAH or BUMMER?

MOOLAH
As usual, January returns
and so does investor money.
Your patience and knowledge
are rewarded.

BUMMER!
Oh no.
The September losses
are the beginning of a crash.
Your stocks plunge even further.
You panic, and you sell!
Bummer.

P/E RATIO
Price/Earnings ratio

Whenever your friends
try to fix you up with a blind date,
there are always certain critical pieces of information
you want to know.
Is he cute? Does he have any weird habits?
Any future potential?
Well, there are certain critical pieces of information
for evaluating a stock.
The P/E ratio is one of them.
It's a corporation's current stock price
divided by its EPS (earnings per share)
for the past twelve months.
XOX is a stock with a high P/E ratio
compared to others in the same industry.
You're considering buying 500 shares of XOX.

Do you or don't you?
Will you or won't you?
Which will it be?
MOOLAH or BUMMER?

MOOLAH
A higher P/E ratio
means investors have higher expectations
for future growth.
And they were right!
The stock price rises
and the 500 shares you bought
bring you a cool profit.

BUMMER!
A higher P/E ratio
means investors have higher expectations
for future growth.

And they were right!
The stock price rises
but you gain zilch
because you sat on the sidelines.
Bummer.

PHISHING

The email from your bank
is one of many in your cluttered Inbox.
As you wrap up a phone call on the speakerphone,
you save the memo you're writing
and simultaneously scan the email.
It's multitasking at its finest.
"Many of you are aware of
the large number of identity-theft attempts",
the email says. "In order to safeguard your account,
we request confirmation of your banking details."
You click on the link in the email.
It takes you to the bank's website.
You notice their famous logo.
As you're about to enter your name and social security number,
it occurs to you this email could be a scam.

Do you or don't you?
Will you or won't you?
Which will it be?
MOOLAH or BUMMER?

MOOLAH
Your skepticism was right on target.
The email is an example of sophisticated phishing,
where a bogus company sends an official looking email
to try and obtain your credit card or banking info.
You call up your bank (the *real* one)
and inquire about the email.
They confirm it's bogus.
You were smart enough to avoid it.

BUMMER!
You enter your banking info
and click "Submit".
Thirteen seconds later,

a sinking feeling creeps into your stomach.
You call up your bank (the *real* one)
and they confirm what you don't want to hear...
the email *is* a scam.
Luckily, the bank freezes your account
so the scammers can't touch it.
But neither can you for a while.
Oh well, a temporary inconvenience
sure beats identity theft.
Bummer.

PORTFOLIO

In the ancient Chinese fighting system of tai chi
you learn how to fight
like many different animals.
You adapt your fighting style
depending on what you're up against.
You can become an eagle against a rat,
or a mongoose against a snake.
There's collective power in being able to
move like so many different animals.
Likewise, when constructing your investment portfolio
you're creating a collection of diverse investments.
As economic and corporate conditions change,
the different "animals" in your portfolio
will generate different returns
so your overall portfolio fares well.

Do you or don't you?
Will you or won't you?
Which will it be?
MOOLAH or BUMMER?

MOOLAH
You crafted a diversified portfolio
with lions, bears, snakes, rabbits
and a whole Noah's Ark of creatures.
Over the long term,
as market conditions rise and fall,
your portfolio thrives.

BUMMER!
Being a bird lover
you fill your portfolio with only birds,
albeit birds of different feathers
(which is your idea of diversification).

Your portfolio is a sitting duck.
Bummer.

PREPAYMENT PENALTY

You and your buddy Roberto are like oil and water.
You believe the early bird always gets the worm,
to which Roberto says, "Mañana."
One day, Roberto surprises you
when he proposes
making one extra mortgage payment each year.
Both of you are doing well in your careers
so have a little extra cash each month.

Do you or don't you?
Will you or won't you?
Which will it be?
MOOLAH or BUMMER?

MOOLAH
It's a great suggestion.
You check to make sure
there's no prepayment penalty,
a fee you'd owe the bank if you
repay the mortgage ahead of schedule.
There isn't!
By making one extra mortgage payment a year,
you shave about a year off your 15 year mortgage.
Sweet.

BUMMER!
It's a great suggestion
but Roberto didn't read the fine print,
which says there's a prepayment penalty
if you pay your mortgage off early.
Bummer.

PRESIDENT'S 3rd YEAR

You and your sweetie are moving in together,
and can't decide which couch to sell.
You then remember it's the
3rd year of the U.S. presidency!
In the past, the S&P 500
(an index fund of the largest 500 stocks)
has risen an average of 19% in this year.
You decide to buy index funds
and give away both couches.
Will you be squatting or lounging?

Do you or don't you?
Will you or won't you?
Which will it be?
MOOLAH or BUMMER?

MOOLAH
Yeah! History repeats itself.
You and your sweetie
end up buying a house together.

BUMMER!
An a-typically bad year.
You break up
but live together out of desperation.
Bummer.

PRIME RATE

You're starting a new business,
a food emporium to cater to pampered kitties.
Kattropolis will retail gourmet feline foods
(salmon blackened in catnip, catnip cookies),
nutritional supplements (vitamins M, E, O and W),
Kattade energy drinks, and other fabulous feline fancies.
You apply for a small business loan to cover the start-up expenses.
The SBA loan officer evaluates your financial history,
then punches some numbers into the computer
to determine at what interest rate
to lend you money.
Prime rate is the interest rate
at which banks lend to their best customers.
What rate will she offer you?

Do you or don't you?
Will you or won't you?
Which will it be?
MOOLAH or BUMMER?

MOOLAH
You have a stellar financial track record
so are considered most creditworthy.
The loan officer gives you her prettiest smile
and offers you an SBA loan at below prime.

BUMMER!
Ouch! A couple of financial blunders
are about to cost you several interest rate points.
The loan officer smiles at you consolingly,
and offers you an SBA loan at well above the prime rate.
Bummer.

PRINCIPAL

The house is fantastic!
5,536 square feet on almost a full acre
with panoramic views!
The mortgage is, well, equally fantastic.
Yup, congratulations on qualifying
for such an impressive mortgage.
What gets you *going* though are the interest payments.
The interest payments are just as beefy
as the principal (the actual amount you're borrowing).
You groan under the weight of your financial obligation.
Racing home from the office after midnight,
you wonder whether it's time to lighten up.

Do you or don't you?
Will you or won't you?
Which will it be?
MOOLAH or BUMMER?

MOOLAH
You sell the house.
What a relief to be free
of those monthly mortgage payments.
And you lose a ton of weight.
Next time, your appetite is smaller.

BUMMER!
Although you choose to lighten up,
your timing is off.
The housing market has softened.
Now, you're imprisoned in your 5,536 square foot castle.
Bummer.

PROFIT = REVENUES - COSTS

In the days of King Arthur
and his Knights of the Round Table,
courtship was very costly.
Today, it's easier.
On a Saturday night date
a man may give his love some flowers,
dinner at a nice restaurant, and take her to a show.
Well, the love pats you receive from your date
are like the "revenues" a business generates,
and your "profit" is your satisfaction level
after you subtract the cost of the date.
If you want bigger profits,
you need to manage costs…
Eat cheapo, pick wildflowers and watch a video.
Or, make sure revenues
are well above costs incurred.
Sir Launcelot was willing to lose *his life*
for Guinevere's love,
a love that met his every desire.
Next Saturday night
how much are you going to pay
for your love pats?

Do you or don't you?
Will you or won't you?
Which will it be?
MOOLAH or BUMMER?

MOOLAH
You give your date a dozen red roses.
The cost may be high, but have no fear!
You are showered with a love
that exceeds your wildest fantasies.
As the sage says,

"A dozen red roses costs more than a single rose,
but you may receive many more petals of love."

BUMMER!
Being the type who thins the toothpaste,
you treat your date likewise.
Alas, the profits are slim.
She ends the date early,
confessing a throbbing headache.
Bummer.

RANDOM WALK THEORY

Out on your morning walk around the block,
you ponder Random Walk Theory
which states that stock prices
rise and fall
for no apparent reason.
This phenomenon vexes you terribly.
In search of an answer
you spend seven years
wandering the plateaus of Upper Tibet,
consulting with innocent children,
yaks, and holy men.
You return with much enlightenment.
How does your portfolio do?

Do you or don't you?
Will you or won't you?
Which will it be?
MOOLAH or BUMMER?

MOOLAH
Your new wisdom and patience serve you well.
The answer is: index funds,
which closely match market performance.
When you hold them over the long term,
history says you'll do well.

BUMMER!
The answer is: give up!
The markets are random
and people are foolish.
Return to Tibet.
Bummer.

RETAIL SALES

Every week, you visit Gigi, your favorite clerk
who works the perfume counter
of your local department store.
She smells exceptionally delicious today,
and you express sympathy
hearing she's not making as many sales as she would like.
Paying for your dozen gift wrapped purchases,
a pang of remorse ripples through your body.
A slowdown in retail sales
suggests a slowdown in the economy.
Do you base your investing
on how many doohickeys others buy?

Do you or don't you?
Will you or won't you?
Which will it be?
MOOLAH or BUMMER?

MOOLAH
You knew that slowing retail sales
mean a slowing economy,
so you wisely invested in defensive stocks
which usually buck the trend.

BUMMER!
You neglected to keep track of retail sales,
and invested too aggressively.
The economy sputters.
You lose a small bundle.
No snowboarding trip for you.
Bummer.

RETURN

You're on a beautiful bike tour
through the wine country.
The bike you're riding is made of Inobtanium,
and is so magical
you decide to buy stock
in the company that makes it,
expecting a good return.
Little do you know
there's a worldwide Inobtanium shortage.

Do you or don't you?
Will you or won't you?
Which will it be?
MOOLAH or BUMMER?

MOOLAH
A replacement for Inobtanium is found,
the stock rises and
you pay for the trip with the dividends.

BUMMER!
The bike tour is wonderful,
but dividends are as skinny as your bike tires
and the return on your investment
is as light as the frame.
Your return home is also light,
as you sell the bike to pay for the flight.
Bummer.

RIGHT OF RESCISSION

As a New Year's present to yourself,
you purchase a health club membership.
Your personal trainer promises you
tight abs, titanium buns
and the meditative calm of a yogi.
Two days later at your weekly knitting group,
you realize your true nature is to knit.
Notwithstanding your desire for titanium buns,
you wonder how much time you'll spend at the gym?
You remember you have the Right of Rescission,
which allows you to void a contract
without any penalty within three days
(United States Consumer Credit Protection Act of 1968).

Do you or don't you?
Will you or won't you?
Which will it be?
MOOLAH or BUMMER?

MOOLAH
The Sage also says,
"Wealth comes to those who finish what they start.
If you can achieve titanium buns,
you will be capable of many more great things."
So, taking the wisdom of the Sage to heart,
you stick with your health club membership.
Lo and behold, your increased vitality
gives you more energy
to devote to your work,
and to knit.

BUMMER!
You take advantage of the Right of Rescission,
and before midnight on the third day,
you null and void the health club contract.

Your lack of follow through reflects the rest of your life,
good intentions fallen by the wayside.
As the Sage says, while pinching your saddlebags,
"Talk is cheap".
Bummer.

RISK

Whenever
your favorite jeans no longer fit,
you go on diet.
The latest fad is the low-carb diet,
a diet that would require you to forgo
your favorite custard-filled donuts.
Being risk averse,
you question how much scientific background
there is to the low-carb diet.
If you exercise more and eat a little less,
wouldn't you lose the same weight
as you would on the low-carb diet
and with less risk?
Or is the risk-return tradeoff such that
with the greater risk of the low-carb diet
you might lose more weight?

Do you or don't you?
Will you or won't you?
Which will it be?
MOOLAH or BUMMER?

MOOLAH
Being risk averse,
you choose the more predictable weight-loss method
of eating less and exercising more.
It may be boring,
but you fit your jeans
while still chomping an occasional donut.

BUMMER!
A majority of your coworkers go low-carb.
They rationalize it can't be overly risky
when so many people are doing it.
Due to lack of sufficient support

the Friday Donut Club is cancelled!
Bummer.

RISK-RETURN TRADEOFF

Sitting at your wireless laptop
watching the NASDAQ,
your mind returns to an email
from your best friend.
In it he quoted the Dalai Lama who said,
"Take into account that great love and
great achievements involve great risk."
As the message echoes in your mind,
you find yourself seeing
an unexpected connection
between this wisdom and
knowledge of the market:
Higher risk stocks may
result in greater returns
but involve great risk.
Less risky investments
tend to bring moderate returns
and a smaller potential for loss.
You decide to give Buddhism a shot
and buy into risky speculative stocks
because of the potentially great returns.
Will the Lama's great wisdom
increase your wealth?

Do you or don't you?
Will you or won't you?
Which will it be?
MOOLAH or BUMMER?

MOOLAH
The Lama's right!
Your great risk brings great returns.
You're finding your inner investor!

BUMMER!
The Lama's right!
You risked and lost it all,
then lost more
by giving up investing entirely.
Bummer.

ROLL OVER

While laboring
at the Teenie Tiny Diaper company,
you participated in their corporate retirement plan.
Now you're moving
to the Super Soaker Undsies company.
What to do with your retirement funds?
"No problem", says the Human Resources Manager,
"just roll it over to another retirement plan.
You can go with
the Super Soaker Undsies retirement plan
or a roll over retirement fund
at a financial services company."

Do you or don't you?
Will you or won't you?
Which will it be?
MOOLAH or BUMMER?

MOOLAH
The roll over goes without a hitch.
You authorize a roll over of your retirement funds
from the Teenie Tiny Diaper company
to the Secure Forever Financial Services company.
There's no time limit for rolling over
from one institution to another.
You continue saving and investing
for a golden tomorrow.
No problemo.

BUMMER!
You procrastinate.
Now more than 60 days have passed
Since the Teenie Tiny Diaper company
cut you a check for your retirement funds,
exceeding the interim roll over period.

Now your Teenie Tiny Diaper retirement money
can't go into another retirement fund
and must be treated as "regular" income.
Instead of the taxes being due
when you retire and withdraw the money,
you'll owe the taxes next April 15th.
Bummer.

ROTH IRA

With music blaring from your iPod,
you're spinning as fast
as your toothpick legs will go.
As you watch the beads of sweat
plop on the crankshaft,
it occurs to you paying taxes
is the opposite of earning interest on your savings.
If you could hold onto
the taxes you pay on your earnings,
you could invest those "taxes" and earn more.
Well, the ROTH IRA lets you
contribute a specified amount (the principal) annually
and withdraw the principal
and your earnings (on the principal)
when you retire...*tax-free.*

Do you or don't you?
Will you or won't you?
Which will it be?
MOOLAH or BUMMER?

MOOLAH
Sounds too good to pass up!
You rip off the earphones,
thoughtfully wipe up the pool of sweat,
and call your finicky financial advisor, Dick.
Dick gives the green light, because you still
meet the maximum annual income allowed
to qualify for a ROTH.
Yeah, tax-free earnings!

BUMMER!
You think there're still many years
before you'll be retiring.
You'd rather go hang with your buddies

than fill out some paperwork.
No ROTH. No tax-free earnings.
Live now. Pay tomorrow.
Bummer.

SEC
(Securities & Exchange Commission)

Sandwiched between
two senior executives at the urinals,
you overhear them bragging
about phony purchase orders
and off-shore accounts.
Oops. You almost miss.
As you fumble with your zipper,
you wonder whether to contact the SEC.
The SEC regulates U.S. financial markets
and protects us against the Gordon Gekko wanna-be's.
Then you remember
all the company stock you own.
Won't the stock drop
if the financial finagling become public,
and with that, your retirement savings?

Do you or don't you?
Will you or won't you?
Which will it be?
MOOLAH or BUMMER?

MOOLAH
You feel torn
about being a whistle blower
but aspire to higher standards.
As it turns out the SEC is
already onto your company.
The guilty executives are replaced
by new managers who clean house.
The stock stays up
and so does your portfolio.

BUMMER!
Gordon Gekko said, "Greed is good".

Well, your greed gets the better of you
so you stay mum.
But there's a leak about the phony accounts,
all the way to the evening news.
The stock drops like a rock
and with it your portfolio.
Bummer.

SECONDARY OFFERINGS

This morning is really starting off on the wrong shoe.
You got in a BIG fight with your sweetie,
missed your commuter train
and now you're stewing in heavy traffic.
As if things couldn't get worse,
a company in your portfolio
is deciding to make a secondary offering.
Though this creation and sale of new stock
can raise money for significant growth and expansion,
it's generally viewed negatively by investors.
Bumper to bumper in the number four lane,
You're about to call your financial advisor, Dick,
when the cell phone rings.
It's your sweetie calling to apologize.
Sweetie or Dick?

Do you or don't you?
Will you or won't you?
Which will it be?
MOOLAH or BUMMER?

MOOLAH
You cut your sweetie off
to call Dick.
She will appreciate
a secure financial future.

BUMMER!
You take the call
and make up with your sweetie,
but miss the window to sell.
As the Sage says,
"Life is full of compromises."
Bummer.

SECURITY ANALYSTS

At the zoo one weekend,
you're at the giraffe exhibit
when you meet Lizst.
Lizst is a senior analyst
with a new securities firm,
"Ana, Lizst, and Tinker".
Lizst is confident of some stocks
and lets you in on it.
You trust the tip, and invest.
Maybe Lizst will turn out to be
the next stock market guru,
and maybe even find her way
onto your breakfast cereal box?

Do you or don't you?
Will you or won't you?
Which will it be?
MOOLAH or BUMMER?

MOOLAH
Lizst was right!
The stocks rose higher than a giraffe's head.
Now you can go to Kenya to see wild giraffes!

BUMMER!
Lizst knew as much
as that giraffe.
You might as well read
giraffe doo-doo for stock tips.
Bummer.

SHORT SQUEEZE

At age eight
you'd eat your dessert
before your meat and potatoes.
Mom 'n Dad didn't mind
as long as you cleaned up your plate.
After all, the end result was the same.
Today, as an investor
you still prefer doing things backwards.
Where most others try to "buy low, sell high",
you're most comfortable when you "sell high, buy low".
This is also known as shorting a stock.
Recently you shorted a tech stock.
Now you're waiting
for the stock price to drop
so you can buy low and take your profit.

Do you or don't you?
Will you or won't you?
Which will it be?
MOOLAH or BUMMER?

MOOLAH
You predicted right.
The stock drops.
You love dessert.

BUMMER!
You predicted wrong.
The stock price rises!
You're caught in a short squeeze!
To avoid losing even more moolah
you must cover your short position.
You have to buy at a higher price
than you sold the stock for.
Bummer.

SOCIALLY CONSCIOUS MUTUAL FUND

There used to be
only one rule you played by:
Win at all costs!
With your investments,
you chose companies with big profits in big markets.
It didn't matter how harmful the effects of their products.
Until, one day, it hit close to home.
Your mom was diagnosed with lung cancer.
Those big fat tobacco companies
that have racked up steady returns
year after year after year,
helping your portfolio grow fat and happy,
You're seriously considering dumping them.

Do you or don't you?
Will you or won't you?
Which will it be?
MOOLAH or BUMMER?

MOOLAH
Instead you invest in
a socially conscious mutual fund,
that invests in companies
with markets and products
not causing any harmful effects.
Initially the returns are less than you're used to,
But as more and more likeminded citizens spread the word,
the returns rival the best of the worst.

BUMMER!
You don't want to take it too personally.
You leave your portfolio just the way it is,
preserving the status quo.
When a big class action lawsuit
hits the tobacco companies,

their profits tank.
Bummer.

STOCK

Carolyn, your well-heeled sorority sister,
inherited stock from her grandparents
on the day she was born.
On her 21st birthday
she was allowed to sell it.
By then, it had tripled in value.
Randy, your coworker, trades stocks excessively,
and goes to a 12 Step program at night.
Linda swears she'll never buy stocks again.
Her retirement account lost most of its value
when the stock market bubble burst.
She's only six years from retirement.
And you?

Do you or don't you?
Will you or won't you?
Which will it be?
MOOLAH or BUMMER?

MOOLAH
You buy stock in the Gotcha Oil 'n Gas company.
It's run by managers with excellent track records,
has high potential profits,
leading products and service,
strong distribution channels
and lotsa sizzle.
Like Carolyn's grandparents,
you buy with a view to the long-term.
And time rewards you.

BUMMER!
You buy some shares in the
Fountain of Youth biotech company.
It's been a strong performer,
but you're too late.

The stock is already way overvalued (overpriced).
Bummer.

SUNK COST

You spent a small fortune
on a gorgeous Persian carpet.
You love its soft silky feel
and intertwining patterns.
Then you meet Tex.
Six weeks into the relationship,
you invite him over to your place.
On the anticipated evening
he suddenly starts sneezing and crying like a baby.
"It's the rug, the #*% rug," he moans,
then hastily apologizes for his language malfunction.
You really like Tex,
but what about your gorgeous Persian rug?

Do you or don't you?
Will you or won't you?
Which will it be?
MOOLAH or BUMMER?

MOOLAH
The carpet is so beautiful
but Tex is more precious to you
than the most gorgeous rug.
You decide to be pragmatic,
choosing to view it as a sunk cost,
a cost already incurred
which is now a thing of the past.
You give the rug away.
You'll get over it.

BUMMER!
Tex is such a catch
but your Persian rug is a truly rare find.
So, much as you love him,
you pass him up.

You'll get over it.
Bummer.

SUPERBOWL EFFECT

The Superbowl party on your 60 foot sailing yacht
is exceptionally successful.
Not only do you make some strategic business contacts,
and acquire a date for next Friday,
but an NFC team wins.
Regardless of how the date goes,
you feel optimistic about the future.
It's been historically a good year
for the markets
when the NFC takes the Superbowl.

Do you or don't you?
Will you or won't you?
Which will it be?
MOOLAH or BUMMER?

MOOLAH
Ya gotta love history!
As predicted, it's a strong year for stocks.
The NFC team won earlier,
and now you do too.

BUMMER!
Unfortunately for you,
this isn't one of those years.
Although the NFC team won, stocks lose.
And so do you.
Bummer.

SHORT SELLING

It's a 4th of July BBQ
at your mom's house.
Your tipsy cousin reveals
that she and some coworkers
are filing a lawsuit against
a big time software company.
Although she is hopelessly
outgunned by their legal army,
blood is thicker than water.
You're considering shorting
the software company's stock
with a mind to buy back
after the stock has dropped.

Do you or don't you?
Will you or won't you?
Which will it be?
MOOLAH or BUMMER?

MOOLAH
By July 10th,
the lawsuit is public
and the stock plummets.
You can now buy it back
at a lower price, and reap a nifty profit.
Hooray for your tipsy cousin!

BUMMER!
And the winner is…
Big time software company.
The lawsuit was dismissed outright.
The company benefits from
the free publicity.
You're forced to buy back

the stock at a higher price.
Bummer.

STOCK SPLITS

You're warming up
for your morning jog one day.
While doing the splits,
your mind wanders
to a stock you own.
The stock has been rising steadily
so the board of directors announces
a 2-for-1 split.
You'll own twice as many shares
at half the previous price.
What do you do?

Do you or don't you?
Will you or won't you?
Which will it be?
MOOLAH or BUMMER?

MOOLAH
The new stocks are in demand
And more investors can afford it at the lower price.
The pre-split run-up in stock price continues.
Your stocks and your running
grow stronger.

BUMMER!
You now own twice as many share
of a stock that peaked yesterday.
Your stock stinks,
and so do your shoes.
Bummer.

STOCKBROKERS

To focus on your true passion, yoga,
you switch to an online discount broker.
You save on commissions
and increase your meditation time,
thereby also attaining a higher financial awareness.
You and your stocks
are manifesting their fullest potential.
"Om Nama Shivaya."
Or are they?

Do you or don't you?
Will you or won't you?
Which will it be?
MOOLAH or BUMMER?

MOOLAH
After 6 months of kundalini stock brokering,
your chakras are
as clear as your debts.
You're in a higher spiritual plane
as you do a yoga pose for "money",
and chant,
"Om, I'm in the money, Om".

BUMMER!
You realize your online company is a sham.
You lose your savings,
but not your Higher Self
as you do a yoga pose for "loss",
and chant,
"Om, I lost it all, Om".
Bummer.

TEASER RATE

She's perched on a barstool,
black stiletto heels
reminiscent of a bygone era,
batting beautiful long eyelashes.
You give her a quick look over.
This is my day, you think,
returning her smile.
You consider approaching.
Is she for real or just a tease?

Do you or don't you?
Will you or won't you?
Which will it be?
MOOLAH or BUMMER?

MOOLAH
Her smile is genuine.
It's the start of a beautiful relationship.

BUMMER!
What a tease!
Her smile is like a teaser rate
on an adjustable-rate mortgage.
It's set low to entice borrowers.
Later, the low rate is replaced
by a much higher market-level rate.
After you approach the lovely lass
she excuses herself to the ladies room.
Her cousin, Prunella, comes up to you.
"Hope you don't mind,
but Kristen had to leave,"
says Prunella, perching herself on the barstool.
It's a classic bait and switch.
Bummer.

TIME VALUE OF MONEY

Your cell phone is beeping.
It's Lizzie, your younger sister,
calling to ask for moolah again.
You've always helped her out,
but this time you ignore the incoming call,
preferring to watch American Idol.
Hey, now she's sending
text messages and video clips!
How rude, you think
and you consider dumping
your gizmo-loaded flip phone.
You're about to turn your phone off,
but wait, what's that her message says?

Do you or don't you?
Will you or won't you?
Which will it be?
MOOLAH or BUMMER?

MOOLAH
"Finally able to repay you after all this time.
You'll have the money this week
plus the interest you would have earned on it,
because a dollar given yesterday
is worth more than a dollar returned today.
Love U forever, Lizzie."
Way to go, Lizzie!

BUMMER!
You open the video attachment
only to see Lizzie
in the driver's seat
of a red convertible.
The message reads, "What a beaut!
Can U help with downpayment?

Love U forever, Lizzie."
Bummer.

VOLATILITY

The stock market has been so volatile recently.
You worry about your riskier investments
careening up and down like a roller coaster.
One of them is Volatile Chemicals Multinational (VCM).
You consider tossing this stock
before it blows up in your face…
so you sell,
but do you catch the market
when the roller coaster is heading up
or down?

Do you or don't you?
Will you or won't you?
Which will it be?
MOOLAH or BUMMER?

MOOLAH
You sell on an upswing
and earn 20% in a day!
You love volatility now!

BUMMER!
You drop the stock on a downswing
and lose 20%.
You hate volatility.
Bummer.

WEAK DOLLAR

You and the guys take a surf trip to Melanesia.
Spending hours at the breaks of Vanuatu and outer Fiji,
you forget about the markets.
The trip even gets better when
you meet Hannah, Elke and Kylli,
Finnish market analysts doing the same.
However, in contrast to your two weeks,
They're on holiday for a year.
Kylli tells you,
"I anticipated a weak US dollar,
so I sold all my American stocks."
Just then, you realize you haven't kept track
of how your investments are doing.

Do you or don't you?
Will you or won't you?
Which will it be?
MOOLAH or BUMMER?

MOOLAH
Fear not.
Kylli's wealth was all inherited.
She's an international trust fund brat
and knows nothing about the US dollar.
Your portfolio is fine.

BUMMER!
Oh no! Kylli was right.
She wasn't just trying to impress you.
While you were surfing in Fiji,
the US dollar has wiped out,
taking your wealth with it.
Bummer.

CONCLUSION

If there were a milestone marker for each topic in this book, then, by making it this far, you've successfully navigated 92 milestones. Congratulations! You're now 92 times more financially savvy than you were before you started your journey to the land of *Moolah or Bummer!*

Now that you know some of the basics of finance and investing, reading the *Wall Street Journal, Fortune, BusinessWeek* or the biz section of your local newspaper will take on a whole new meaning. You'll understand the content because the financial jargon won't get in your way. That's good news for you and bad news for anyone who tries to pull the wool over your eyes.

Still thirsty for more? Well, although your journey to the land of *Moolah or Bummer!* has come to an end, your quest for a higher level of financial consciousness has only just begun. Turn to the next section for a recommended list of financial publications that can take you further into the world of business, economics and finance.

And remember, as the Sage says, "A journey of a thousand miles begins with the first step. Happy is the person who, at each step, chooses *Moolah*, not *Bummer!*"

FOR FURTHER READING

David Bach, *Smart Women Finish Rich* (Broadway, 1999); *Smart Couples Finish Rich* (Broadway, 2002).

Fred Brock, *Live Well On Less Than You Think: The New York Times Guide to Achieving Your Financial Freedom* (Times Books, 2005); *Retire On Less Than You Think* (Times Books, 2004).

David Gardner, Tom Gardner, *The Motley Fool Investment Guide* (Fireside, 2001).

David Gardner, Tom Gardner, *The Motley Fool Personal Finance Workbook: A Foolproof Guide to Organizing Your Cash and Building Wealth* (Fireside, 2003).

David Gardner, Tom Gardner, Selena Maranjian, *The Motley Fool Investment Guide for Teens: 8 Steps to Having More Money Than Your Parents Ever Dreamed Of* (Fireside, 2002).

Robert T. Kiyosaki with Sharon L. Lechter, *Rich Dad Poor Dad* (TechPress, 1997).

Beth Kobliner, *Get a Financial Life: Personal Finance in Your Twenties and Thirties* (Fireside, 2000).

Kenneth M. Morris, Virginia B. Morris, *The Wall Street Journal Guide to Understanding Money and Investing* (Fireside, 2004).

Suze Orman, *9 Steps to Financial Freedom: Practical and Spiritual Steps so You Can Stop Worrying* (Three Rivers Press, 2000).

Juliet B. Schor, *The Overspent American* (Perennial, 1999).

Andrew Tobias, *The Only Investment Guide You'll Ever Need* (Harvest Books, 1998).

Eric Tyson, *Personal Finance for Dummies* (For Dummies, 2003); *Mortgages for Dummies* (For Dummies, 1999); *Investing for Dummies* (Wiley, 2002); *Mutual Funds for Dummies* (For Dummies, 2001).

Jane Bryant Quinn, *Making the Most of Your Money* (Simon & Schuster, 1997).

For information on specialized topics

Christine Benz, Peter Di Teresa, Russel Kinnel, Don Phillips, *The Morningstar Guide to Mutual Funds: 5-Star Strategies for Success* (John Wiley & Sons, 2003).

John C. Bogle, *Common Sense on Mutual Funds: New Imperatives for the Intelligent Investor* (Wiley, 2000).

Warren Buffet, Warren E. Buffet, Lawrence A. Cunningham, *The Essays of Warren Buffet: Lessons for Corporate America* (The Cunningham Group, 2001).

Phillip A. Fisher, Kenneth L. Fisher, *Common Stocks and Uncommon Profits and Other Writings* (John Wiley and Sons, 2003).

Benjamin Graham, Spencer B. Meredith, *The Interpretation of Financial Statements* (HarperBusiness, 1998)

Benjamin Graham with Jason Zweig, *The Intelligent Investor, Revised Edition* (HarperBusiness, 2003).

Robert S. Griswold, *Property Management for Dummies* (For Dummies, 2001).

J.K. Lasser Institute, *J.K. Lasser's Your Income Tax 2005: For Preparing Your 2004 Tax Return* (John Wiley & Sons, 2004, updated annually)

Peter Lynch, John Rothchild, *One Up on Wall Street: How to Use What You Already Know to Make Money in the Market* (Simon & Shuster, 2000).

Liz Pulliam Weston, *Your Credit Score: How to Fix, Improve, and Protect the 3-Digit Number That Shapes Your Financial Future* (Prentice Hall, 2004).

FINANCIAL WEBSITES AND PUBLICATIONS

This list includes some of the major financial and business websites and the corresponding parent organization or publication.

Financial Information and News

http://finance.yahoo.com	Yahoo
http://moneycentral.msn.com	CNBC
www.marketwatch.com	CBS, Dow Jones
http://money.cnn.com	CNN, Money
www.fool.com	Motley Fool
http://online.wsj.com	The Wall Street Journal
www.economist.com	The Economist
www.investors.com	Investors Business Daily
www.fortune.com	Fortune
www.businessweek.com	BusinessWeek
http://online.barrons.com	Barrons
www.inc.com	Inc.
www.hoovers.com	Hoovers

www.bloomberg.com	Bloomberg
http://reuters.com	Reuters
www.smartmoney.com	Smart Money
www.forbes.com	Forbes

Stock, Mutual Fund, Bond and Financial Research

www.standardandpoors.com	Standard and Poors
www.zacks.com	Zacks Investment Research
www.valueline.com	Value Line
www.bondsonline.com	BondsOnline Group
www.afajof.org	American Finance Association
www.aaii.com	American Association of Individual Investors
www.fma.org	Financial Management Association
www.cepr.net	Center for Economic Policy Research

Stock Exchanges and Regulators

www.sec.gov	Securities and Exchange Commission
www.nasd.com	National Association of Securities Dealers
www.nyse.com	New York Stock Exchange
www.nasdaq.com	NASDAQ Exchange
www.amex.com	American Stock Exchange
www.cboe.com	Chicago Board Options Exchange

Other Useful Websites

www.cardratings.com	Credit card ratings
www.bankrate.com	Consumer information on financial products
www.banksite.com	Online calculators
www.cfpboard.org	Certified Financial Planners
www.naic.org	National Association of Insurance Commissioners

Note: The author is not liable for any products, services or content in any of the above publications, websites and organizations.

AUTHOR BIOGRAPHY

Moget Africa received her B.S. degree from Stanford University and her MBA from the University of San Diego. She has over fifteen years experience in business, new product development and marketing for Fortune 500 and start-up companies. The author enjoys investing and money management, and is the recipient of numerous patent awards.

YOUR FEEDBACK IS WELCOME

If you would like to send feedback on *Moolah or Bummer! A Humorous Look at Finance and Investing* you can email the author at MogetAfrica@yahoo.com or www.MoolahorBummer.com. However, please do not be offended if your email is not acknowledged with a reply. For liability reasons, please do not contact the author regarding any financial or investment recommendations, products, services or advice.

0-595-34431-3